BUSH MEDICINE
Healing from Country

By Vikki McIntyre

Illustrated by Luna Undra

Library For All Ltd.

Bush medicine knowledge

Have you ever wondered how our people stayed strong and healthy long before chemists and hospitals existed?

The answer lies in the powerful knowledge of bush medicine, passed down through generations of Aboriginal and Torres Strait Islander communities. Elders hold this special knowledge and continue to share it today, helping us heal and stay connected to our Country.

3

Tea tree oil – Nature's antiseptic

Imagine you're exploring the bush and accidentally get a small cut or scratch. Our old people knew exactly what to use in these situations. Tea tree leaves, crushed and rubbed gently onto your skin, clean wounds and stop infections.

It's nature's antiseptic! Today, many people around the world use tea tree oil for cuts, grazes, and even to help clear pimples.

Lemon myrtle — Soothing coughs and colds

During colder months, catching coughs or colds can make us feel miserable. Our Elders taught us to use the fragrant lemon myrtle leaves, boiling them gently to make a healing tea.

Drinking this tea eases coughs and colds, helping our bodies recover quickly. Lemon myrtle grows in Australia's eastern rainforests and can also flavour food, keeping us healthy inside and out.

Emu bush – Healing skin problems

Dry skin, eczema, or itchy rashes can be uncomfortable. For thousands of years, Aboriginal communities from Central Australia have used emu bush leaves to heal such skin issues.

Boiling the leaves and applying the cooled liquid to the affected skin is soothing. Emu bush helps skin heal naturally, reducing irritation and inflammation. You'll find emu bush growing in desert and dry regions, showing the deep connection between plants and the places they thrive.

Kakadu plum – Boosting immunity

Did you know the Kakadu plum has the highest level of vitamin C of any fruit in the world? Aboriginal people from the Northern Territory and Western Australia have known about this special fruit for generations. Eating Kakadu plums helps strengthen our immune system, protecting us from illness.

Today, the Kakadu plum is famous worldwide for its healing powers and is used in creams, foods, and vitamins.

Gumbi Gumbi – Strengthening bodies

Gumbi Gumbi, a powerful plant found mainly in Queensland, has long been used by our mob to strengthen bodies and help fight sickness.

Many communities boil the leaves and drink them as a tea to support health, reduce fevers, and assist with recovery from illnesses. Gumbi Gumbi reminds us how important plants can be in keeping us strong and well.

13

Lemongrass — The pain-relief medicine of the bush

We have native lemongrass that grows in the drier parts of the country. The grass can be made into a tea you can drink to help treat diarrhoea, coughs, colds and sore throats.

But that's not all! The roots can be crushed up and rubbed directly onto the skin to treat rashes and sores.

Scientists recently did some more research on native lemongrass and found it can also help with headaches and migraines! It works just like some western pain-relief medicines.

Our way – Healing mind and body together

In our culture, healing isn't just about treating sickness in the body. It's about caring for the mind and spirit too.

Our mob understand that the mind, body, and Country are deeply connected. When we use bush medicine, we don't just help physical symptoms, we also support emotional and spiritual wellbeing. Elders teach that spending time on Country, gathering plants, and learning from nature helps heal sadness, worry, and stress.

Bush medicine reminds us we are part of something bigger, giving us balance and harmony in our lives.

Keeping knowledge alive

Learning about bush medicine helps us respect and care for Country. It connects us with our ancestors, keeping their wisdom alive for future generations. Next time you're out bush, take a closer look at the plants around you. Each one holds a special story, and may have powerful healing properties waiting to be shared.

DID YOU KNOW?

You should never eat or put anything on your skin if you are not sure what it is. Always have an adult with you.

Talk with Elders and knowledgeable community members before using bush medicines. They can guide you to use them safely and respectfully.

19

Bush medicine vs western medicine: A comparison

Let's look at some everyday examples to compare bush medicines with western medicines.

Health issue	Bush medicine example	Western medicine example
Cleaning wounds	Tea tree oil	Antiseptic
Coughs and colds	Lemon myrtle tea	Cough syrup
Skin irritations	Emu bush wash	Hydrocortisone cream
Vitamin C boost	Kakadu plum	Vitamin supplements
General wellbeing	Gumbi Gumbi tea	Multivitamin tablets
Headaches and sore throats	Native lemongrass	Pain-relief medicine

21

Photo Credits

Page	Attribution
Cover	Jose Maria Barres Manuel/alamy.com
Pages 2–3	xavierarnau/istockphoto.com
Page 4	narvikk/istockphoto.com
Page 6	lynnebeclu/istockphoto.com
Page 8	Jose Maria Barres Manuel/alamy.com
Page 10	Leanne Atherton/austockphoto.com
Page 12	Excitations/alamy.com
Page 15	y-studio/istockphoto.com
Pages 18–19	JohnnyGreig/istockphoto.com

You can use these questions to talk about this book with your family, friends and teachers.

What did you learn from this book?

Describe this book in one word. Funny? Scary? Colourful? Interesting?

How did this book make you feel when you finished reading it?

What was your favourite part of this book?

Download the Library For All Reader app from libraryforall.org

About the author

Vikki McIntyre was born in Sydney and grew up in the western suburbs. Her ancestral Country is the south coast of New South Wales. She descends from the saltwater people of the Dharawal language group. Vikki is happiest when she can feel sand under her feet and smell saltwater in the air.

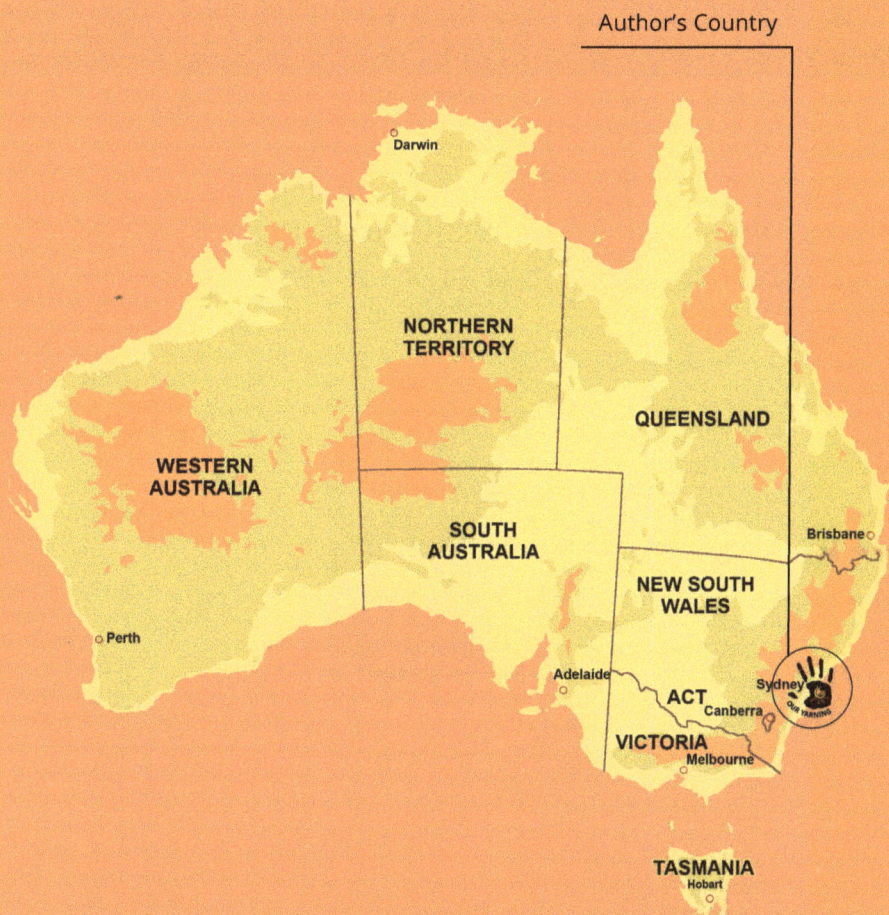

Author's Country

Darwin

NORTHERN
TERRITORY

QUEENSLAND

WESTERN
AUSTRALIA

SOUTH
AUSTRALIA

Brisbane

NEW SOUTH
WALES

Perth

Adelaide

Sydney

ACT
Canberra

VICTORIA
Melbourne

TASMANIA
Hobart

Our Yarning

The Our Yarning collection aligns with the Australian Curriculum through the Cross-Curriculum Priorities — Aboriginal and Torres Strait Islander Histories and Cultures. The collection provides an authentic opportunity for learning and embedding Aboriginal and Torres Strait Islander perspectives because it is written by Aboriginal and Torres Strait Islander people.

We know that children learn better, and enjoy reading more, when they see themselves in the stories, characters and illustrations of the books they read.

To download the app, visit the Google Play Store or Apple Store and search 'Our Yarning'.

libraryforall.org

You're reading Upper Primary

Learner – Beginner readers
Start your reading journey with short words, big ideas and plenty of pictures.

Level 1 – Rising readers
Raise your reading level with more words, simple sentences and exciting images.

Level 2 – Eager readers
Enjoy your reading time with familiar words, but complex sentences.

Level 3 – Progressing readers
Develop your reading skills with creative stories and some challenging vocabulary.

Level 4 – Fluent readers
Step up your reading skills with playful narratives, new words and fun facts.

Middle Primary – Curious readers
Discover your world through science and stories.

Upper Primary – Adventurous readers
Explore your world through science and stories.

Library For All is an Australian not for profit organisation with a mission to make knowledge accessible to all via an innovative digital library solution. Visit us at libraryforall.org

Bush Medicine: Healing from Country

First published 2025

Published by Library For All Ltd
Email: info@libraryforall.org
URL: libraryforall.org

This book was made possible by the generous contributions of GSK.

Our Yarning logo design by Jason Lee, Bidjipidji Art

Original illustrations by Luna Undra

Bush Medicine: Healing from Country
McIntyre, Vikki
ISBN: 978-1-923594-12-8
SKU04962

www.ingramcontent.com/pod-product-compliance
Lightning Source LLC
Chambersburg PA
CBHW042341040426
42448CB00019B/3367